Rock Your Happy

Reconnect, Realign, and Rediscover YOU again!

JENNIFER SHRECKENGOST

Copyright © 2018 Jennifer Shreckengost

All rights reserved.

ISBN-13: 978-0-692-09590-4

To you.

You have bravely carried the weight of everyone else's load; it's time to nurture yourself and blossom.

CONTENTS

	Acknowledgments	i
	Prologue	iii
	Introduction	1
1	Uncovering Your True Story	1
2	Discovering the Limiting Beliefs That Are Holding You Back	11
3	Releasing Our Fears	23
4	Embracing Vulnerability	39
5	Building a Foundation of Self-Love, Care, and Compassion	51
6	Aligning with Your Core Values	71
7	Designing the Framework for Rocking Your Happy!	91
8	Setting Your Goals for Moving Forward	131
9	Secret Granddaddy of Them All	141
10	So, Now What?	143

ACKNOWLEDGMENTS

This book began as a tiny thought, and slowly, over time, grew into what's here for you today.

First and foremost, thank you to my best friend and husband, Mike, who is always in my corner. Your constant support and encouragement have allowed me to create a truly aligned life, pursuing what I've been called to do, and for that I am forever grateful.

For understanding my evenings and long nights at the computer, I'd like to thank my children, Austin, Conner, Jackson, Cody, and Lainey. Always pursue your passions, even when the world tells you otherwise.

To my parents, for putting up with my crazy entrepreneurial journey even when you don't understand what I'm doing. And to my sister as well; who is the last to know but always gives unconditional support.

This book would not have been possible without the support and encouragement of my editor, book coach, and friend, Dr. Beth Brombosz. Her selfless guidance, assistance, and patience allowed me to bring my idea to fruition; words cannot express my gratitude for her.

To my three closest friends, Amber M., Lanetta W., and Amber C., who've watched my transformation first-hand and are always there with candid advice, an ear to listen, a shoulder to cry on, a bottle of wine, and steadfast cheers and spirit fingers.

To Cover Designs by James, GoOnWrite.com, thank you for creating a book cover that captures that essence of the message within these pages.

And finally, to the women I've had the honor to work with, who have followed me on this transformational journey. It's for you that I wake in the morning and push through even when they tell me no. Watching you transform your own lives, that's what fills me up.

PROLOGUE

If you're reading this book, there's a spark that's craving more, even if it's the tiniest of dull embers inside you, it's there nonetheless. My very first message to you is twofold: listen to that spark, and do so without guilt. As women we've spent so many years quieting that inner voice, dulling that spark, pushing it aside because it wasn't our time. Our focus was on others first: our kids, our spouse, our jobs, our household duties, all the things we were raised to think were the 'proper' things for women to focus on. While we've gotten better about things like self-care and compassion over the years, there's still this cloud of guilt that lays nearby, like a morning fog lingering, when we begin to think about putting our needs on the front burner.

When I ask the women I work with what's holding them back from feeling completely happy and fulfilled, here's what I hear:

I should be happy with what I already have.

Life is good, I'm being selfish for wanting more.

Making others happy is should be focusing on.

I've ready every book out there. Nothing is going to change This is as good as it gets.

I can't figure out why I feel disconnected. I just do, and I feel bad for feeling this way.

I don't even know what life could look like outside of being a mom or wife.

It's been so long since I focused on me; I don't even know where to start.

I need to put my family first before anything I want.

Honestly, I've lost who I really am over the years.

I created this book after working with clients inside the Rock Your Happy program. After seeing their transformations, I knew it had the ability to change women's lives. But, I also knew, after countless conversations with women, that not everyone was ready for intimate, one-on-one coaching inside a program like Rock Your Happy. I also knew that so much of what we're wanting starts with the inner game, yet we only turn to outside solutions, like books, podcasts, or articles. Happiness is an inside job. The challenge is that we don't know what we don't know, so I created this book to help women dip their toes into the pool of possibilities. I also created some amazing bonuses to help make this book as valuable as possible. To access your book bonuses, worth almost $500, make sure you head over to www.jennifershreckengost.com/bookbonuses.

My hope for you as you read this book is that you realize you can absolutely reconnect, realign, and rediscover YOU again, in turn creating a more balanced, fulfilled life! You can pursue your passions and still be an excellent mother. You can make time for you and still be a loving wife and mother. You can change careers and not feel guilty about those college degrees you're no longer using. You can take time to focus on your own emotional wellness and not be seen as selfish. You can have it all, as cliché as that may sound. It truly is possible to have a fulfilled life, one that lights you up, that sets your soul on fire, and that, my friend, is my wish for you.

Peace, Love, and Light,

Jennifer

INTRODUCTION

Somewhere along the way you've lost yourself. Among the hustle and bustle of raising a family, climbing the corporate ladder, nurturing your spouse, and taking on all the things like bills, and dinner, and laundry, you've slowly lost yourself. As a child, you may have shouted out to the world amazing aspirations like, "I'm going to be an astronaut!" without even a hint of doubt. Yet, somehow along the way you filed into order, onto a conveyor belt like a good Stepford wife, and joined the lemmings on society's path towards what it defines as a fulfilled life: college + career + marriage + mortgage + 2.5 kids = a Fulfilled Life.

Except, what if that's not our fulfilled life? What if that 20+ year banking career pays the bills, but we're slowly dying inside? What if we love Johnny and Suzie, more than life itself, but we secretly daydream of pursuing our own passions? What if those shiny college degrees hanging on the wall actually are the exact opposite of what you truly want to be doing? Despite the kids, who you absolutely adore, despite your spouse, who you absolutely love, despite the career you built with your blood, sweat, and tears (literally), you still can't help but feel like something is missing, followed by feeling like a royal a-hole for feeling this way.

It's okay, because you're not alone. The fact that you feel like something is missing does not mean you're an ungrateful jerk. It simply means there is room for realignment, room for small changes, room for creating your most fulfilled life. You can absolutely press the reset button on life, at any stage or age. We only get one shot at this life, and we need to take full advantage of our time on this spinning rock. Not someday. Not when we retire at 65. Now. It's time to create a life that sets your soul on fire, a life that feels aligned with your mind, body, and soul. Are you ready?

This book isn't designed to just talk at you, I want to talk with you and guide you, providing you with actionable steps you can put in place now. The goal is half inspiration, and half life-changing action steps.

Before we get started, you're going to get a taste of your first life-changing action step. This book complements the Rock Your Happy Program, which is my flagship program. The Rock Your Happy Program is the starting point for making any change in our lives. Before we can reach that finish line, before we can create any substantial, lasting change within our lives, before we can find ourselves again, we must first take a hard look at our present situation. We need to do a temperature check of sorts on where we are now in relation to living our fulfilled life.

Life-Changing Action

I believe our fulfilled life revolves around five core life areas:

- Personal
- Emotional
- Spiritual
- Physical
- Professional

Each of these five core areas affects our relationships, our happiness, and our overall fulfillment in life. Inside each of these core life areas are our core desired feelings. When our core desired feelings are not aligned with our core values, things get out of whack. Picture a game of double-dutch. You have two ropes, two handlers, and one person jumping in the middle. In order for it to work, each part has to be in sync. The handlers have to be in sync, which makes the ropes move in sync, and then the jumper must be in sync with the rhythm of the ropes. It's the same with our core life areas. If our health is out of sync, our inner self may be thrown off. If our career is out of sync, our health and adventure may be thrown off.

Let's take a temperature check on the alignment of your core life areas.

Consider how you currently {FEEL} in each of these areas. I want you to think deeply on this, but don't overthink or try to force a good feeling if it's not there. I want you to identify the real, raw true feelings that would currently describe how you feel in each of your five core life areas. If you need to look up descriptive words, do so. What emotion or emotions do you feel most often on any given day? Any given week? Are there emotions that come up more often than others? For example, if you feel stressed or overwhelmed daily, those may be two of your chosen descriptive words for one or more core life areas. Sit with each of the core life areas below and reflect upon what emotions surface daily and weekly for you in each area. For each of the five core life areas below, choose the THREE most powerful and accurate descriptive words (adjectives) that would best describe how you currently {FEEL} in each area.

- Personal
- Emotional
- Spiritual
- Physical
- Professional

This is your starting point. Embrace it. It's okay to admit you're unhappy in any of these areas. If you're reading this, you're ready to take action. Let's get this party started!

Repeat this mantra: I choose to live fully without regret, guilt, or shame.

1 UNCOVERING YOUR TRUE STORY

During my late 20s and early 30s I went through a very tumultuous time in my life. I could call it rock bottom, but the truth is, year 29 was just the start to several years at rock bottom. I carried the burden of shame and guilt during these times, and it ultimately changed who I was. I let shame and guilt consume me. I veered away from my core values, from who I truly was. I hid from my story rather than embracing it and honoring it. I lost my self-confidence, I lost my joy, I lost me. Rather than unpackaging and processing those feelings, I shoved them to the back of my mind. I had four kids to raise, a career to ultimately rebuild, rent to pay, groceries to buy; I had

ZERO time to worry about silly feelings of shame and guilt. I told myself to "get over it" and pushed forward. Sound familiar?

The challenge (I like to use the word challenge instead of problem) with this type of behavior is that ultimately you cannot truly create the life you've been craving until you honor your stories and do the unpacking and processing of those feelings. Believe it or not, your subconscious mind is one powerful beast. You only consciously use a tiny portion of your mind; the rest is driven by your subconscious.

The best visualization I can give you for this is to think of an iceberg. We've all seen those images of an iceberg where on the surface we see what looks like a tiny piece of an iceberg, but beneath the surface there's a huge, massive chunk of ice more than five times the size of what we see. That giant piece beneath the surface? That's your subconscious mind. Your actions, decisions, and fears are driven by your subconscious mind. Just like the poor Titanic, if you don't honor what's sitting below the surface, you will sink, and sink fast.

As humans we like to deny (ignore) this fact, because we like to live on the assumption that we are in control. Where are my fellow control freaks?? Sorry, I hate to break it to you, but you're not driving this bus, your subconscious mind is. However, you can choose not to be like Captain Smith of the Titanic. You can choose to honor the power of your subconscious mind and dive into what it's telling you.

We all have stories, starting from childhood. Little Johnny on the playground who called you names, watching Mom and Dad fight over money, teenage heartbreak, your boss who told you that you weren't qualified, divorce, abuse; the list goes on and on. Every single event within your life is part of a story, which has subsequently solidified some form of a limiting belief within you. As much as we think (or attempt to convince ourselves) that we're over such events, the truth of the matter is that the seed of this limiting belief was planted within your subconscious mind without you even realizing it. These seeds then begin to grow into strong limiting beliefs, which then begin to control our actions.

Perhaps there was a time when you didn't go for a promotion because you were afraid of not getting it. The thought of being rejected brought up feelings of failure, so you decided not to even apply just to avoid the possibility of rejection. I once worked with a client who was terribly afraid to share some real, raw emotions she was experiencing with her husband, even though mentally she could visualize herself doing so. She wanted to talk to him, she could pep talk herself into preparing for the conversation, but when it came time she bottled up. She couldn't get over the feeling of him possibly disagreeing with her, or not understanding what she was trying to say. For her, that type of vulnerable conversation was equivalent to rejection and a feeling that she was not being good enough. Maybe you're self-sabotaging your health and wellness even though you know what to do to improve. No matter how much you desperately want to change, you always swing back to where you're currently at, miserable and unhappy.

If any of these sounded a little too familiar and you were shouting, "OMG, YES!" then your subconscious beliefs are driving the bus. Now, before you start to rationalize any of the above with statements like, "I can't change jobs; I have bills to pay," or "I didn't go for the promotion because I didn't want it anyway," take a moment to commit to changing your thought process. Those statements are your conscious mind attempting to rationalize these decisions in order to make you feel "okay." In order to create the change you're looking for, you must commit to opening your mind and changing how you view your thoughts and choices. This is a judgement free zone; no need to start defending those statements above. Deal?

What if I told you the reason(s) for any of those actions listed above are most likely tied to one of the many seeds of limiting beliefs planted in your subconscious mind along your life roadmap? These seeds create strong limiting beliefs, and these limiting beliefs then become deeply embedded within us, rooted down like strong oak tree. The seeds for these beliefs have been planted along the way through your experiences, your relationships, and your interactions. In order to begin finding yourself once again, and to create that change you've been longing for, you must first peel back the layers of the onion, examine your stories, and embrace them. To uncover these limiting beliefs, you must go to the root; you must uncover where they started. I want to note that when I use the word belief, I'm referring to our internal beliefs about ourselves, i.e. I'm not good enough for that job, I'll never lose weight, I'm terrible with money, etc. These are the beliefs that are rooted into our subconscious through life experiences. I want you to be open to being vulnerable in this exercise. Being able to write down your stories is the first step in uncovering where your limiting beliefs and fears began.

Life-Changing Action

Set aside 15-30 minutes of uninterrupted time. Grab your journal, or download the workbook that accompanies this book at www.jennifershreckengost.com/bookbonuses. Get comfortable inside a safe place, and allow yourself to freely explore what comes up as you go through this activity.

Consider significant events that have happened in your life: childhood (birth to pre-teen), teenage years, and adult (20+). Significant events could include any of the following:

- Discoveries
- Tragedies
- Meaningful Memories
- Influential People
- Traumatic Experiences
- Careers
- Schooling
- Successes
- Failures
- Loss
- Wins
- Role Models
- Relationships
- Heartbreak
- Tragedy
- Accomplishments

For each of these, consider both positive and negative experiences. What emotions did you experience? What experiences or relationships brought you great joy? What experiences or relationships still brings up regret and a feeling of shame? Freely write down what comes up when you think about each of these significant events.

Consider the roles that different family members in your life have played and how they may have impacted you, either positively or negatively. This might be Mom, Dad, siblings, aunts, uncles, grandparents, cousins, or other extended family. Write down any significant stories from this area of your life.

Visualize these significant events within your life and draw upon what feelings and emotions came up when you do this. Consider how they may be tied to any of your current beliefs. Did your parents set any examples or say anything that has affected how you view your career now? Are you carrying around beliefs that were ingrained within you as a child by listening to your relatives? For example, "You have to go to college to be successful," or, "Money doesn't come easy."

The purpose of these activities is to help you uncover all your stories. We tend to try to focus only on the highlight reel of our life. You think that if you don't talk about the dark chapters of your stories, they don't exist. Unfortunately, you must be brave and own all of your stories. Divorce, abuse, neglect, addiction, whatever those dark chapters may be, you must own them as part of who you are today. Don't be afraid to call them out; there's no room for shame on your path towards creating your fulfilled life. Embrace you, all of you, because this is where the magic begins to happen.

Repeat this mantra: Every chapter of my story is a valuable piece of who I am today.

2 DISCOVERING THE LIMITING BELIEFS THAT ARE HOLDING YOU BACK

Have you ever sat in a meeting at work and wanted so badly to answer a question or give your opinion, but you refrain from speaking up? This was me, to a T! I would sit in meetings at work and never speak up, never share my opinion, even when I wanted to so badly. Why? Because of one reason…what if I was (dare I say it) wrong?

I wasn't always like this. In fact, my freshman year of high school I was voted Class President, beating out a candidate who everyone thought had the position in the bag. However, over the years, throughout high school, college, interactions, and relationships, the more I spoke up, the more someone quieted me, and the more I retreated.

Instead of rebelling against this, each of these interactions planted a limiting belief onto my subconscious. A limiting belief that I wasn't good enough. That providing the "wrong" answer equaled "not good enough." It wasn't as though someone directly called me out. I never experienced sharing in a group and someone yelling at me, "You're wrong, therefore you're not good enough." No, you see it's not that black and white. Instead, what happened was I shared a thought and someone laughed. I shared and idea and the whole group disagreed. I proposed a solution and it failed. Each of these instances fed into the creation of a strong limiting belief, If I'm wrong, I'm not good enough. I'm a failure. Fast-forward 20 years and I'd pretty much all but zipped my mouth shut in any environment that did not feel safe (and let me tell you, those safe environments were few and far between).

Limiting beliefs are sneaky. They slowly creep into your subconscious, like weeds in your garden. Have you ever planted a garden or flower bed, stood there so proud of its beauty, only to be shocked in horror a week later when you look out and it's flooded with ugly weeds? It's the same with your thoughts. If you don't weed the garden of your mind, regularly processing and throwing out thoughts that don't serve you, you end up with an overgrown jungle of limiting beliefs. That's why doing this type of work on your mindset is so very important. As I previously mentioned, you love to think you're in control, especially of your thoughts. Sadly, your subconscious mind is driving this bus so it's best to show her the respect she deserves.

I know there are some of you reading this and saying to yourself, "I'm good, none of those things in my past bother me today." If that's truly the case, then I applaud you. But for those of you that aren't quite sure, take a look at the list of thoughts below and see if you relate to any.

- I'm not an expert.
- Nobody cares what I have to say.
- I didn't work hard enough on this.
- I'm not worth it.
- I don't deserve [money, recognition,

success].
- I don't have time.
- People will judge me.
- I'm not a [numbers, business] person.
- The people who are successful in this are out of my league.
- I'm not going to be successful, so there's no point in trying.
- I'm too old.
- I'm too young.
- I don't have the willpower.
- I'm just not motivated.
- I can't do that.
- There is no point.
- I can't afford that.
- That's just not "me."

Sound familiar? Yeah, I thought so. At some point we all have limiting beliefs that creep in. They control our decision-making, our careers, our relationships…just about everything. In almost every struggle you'll find some sort of deep-rooted limiting belief. The bad news is, they're going to always creep back in, just like those pesky weeds in your garden. However, the good news is we always have the ability to reverse those beliefs and get rid of them.

I won't tell you that you're going to miraculously rid your conscious and subconscious mind of all limiting beliefs, never to return. Sorry, there's not a Roundup weed killer for limiting beliefs. It's a continual process, and the key to winning that battle is awareness.

A client I recently worked with came to this realization after a few weeks into the Rock Your Happy Program. After doing several weeks' worth of activities and coaching sessions with me, she came to the realization that it's not so much about preventing those thoughts from coming in, but instead having a crystal-clear awareness of when it's happening.

I gave her the analogy of viewing her thoughts from an outsider's perspective, as if she's standing outside of her body and watching exactly what's happening. When you do this, you can see the trigger event, see the reaction, and become aware of the resurfacing of a limiting belief. When you see it happen, you can immediately do the work to reverse it. It was during one of our coaching sessions when the light bulb went off! "Ohhhh, so it's more about awareness and knowing when it's

happening in order to immediately reverse it."
BINGO! She hit the nail on the head.

Life-Changing Action

So how do we get rid of these nasty limiting beliefs and start to become aware of when they rear their ugly heads? We start by simply paying attention to the chatter we have going on upstairs in connection with our five core life areas. What limiting beliefs are you whispering to yourself on a daily basis? What limiting beliefs are driving your decision-making bus?

After completing this exercise, one client I worked with was in shock after uncovering many, many limiting beliefs. What she thought were just simple decisions, she quickly realized were deep-seated limiting beliefs holding her back. She was a single woman, living on her own, and she prided herself on not asking for help. No matter how overwhelmed she was, she didn't want to ask for help. She uncovered that although she thought was just her being a strong, independent woman, she actually had a deep-seated belief that she couldn't ask for help because that meant she was weak and a burden on others, which was also connected to shame.

Spend a day or two reflecting on decisions you make and the content of your self-talk. Write down words and decisions you noticed and then move into a 5-10 minute free write session to summarize it all.

5 - 10 Minute Free Write Session

- Grab a pen.
- Set a time for anywhere from 5 - 10 minutes.
- Just write - write down all of your beliefs that come to mind when you think about your five core life areas.

Don't think, don't process, don't give your conscious thinking mind time to step in. Just continually write until the timer goes off.

Using the list of limiting beliefs you came up with, create a chart like the one shown here. Or, download the workbook companion for this exercise at www.jennifershreckengost.com/bookbonuses.

Limiting Belief	What evidence do you have that _disproves_ that belief?	Your new belief - the opposite of your limiting belief

In the left column, write down every limiting belief that came to mind. Then, write down evidence that you have that disproves that limiting belief. For example, if I have a limiting belief that "I'm terrible at managing money," I'm going to think of all the instances where I could disprove that belief. Maybe I paid off a few bills lately, maybe my checking account stayed in the green and not the red, or maybe I paid extra on a credit card bill. Those are all examples that would disprove my limiting belief that I'm terrible at managing money. Then, you're going to write a new belief, which should essentially be the opposite of your limiting belief.

Example:

Limiting Belief - I'm terrible at managing money.

Evidence that Disproves This - I paid off two extra bills this month and still had money left over. I put additional money into savings.

New Belief - I am capable of successfully managing money, or my money management skills improve every day.

These new beliefs can become your daily affirmations or mantras. Doing so will help you keep your mental garden cleaned up and only pumping out positive beliefs, rather than holding you back with limiting beliefs.

One additional note on writing new beliefs. The

key to reversing our limiting beliefs is to not only create a new belief, but to create a new belief for where we are right now. What I mean by this is, if we create a new belief that doesn't feel good, doesn't sit well with us, or that doesn't feel quite in reach just yet, then it won't stick. So, we start from where we are right now and then as we continue to grow, we continue to create new beliefs. You can't force a new belief; you must slowly grow into it.

Here's an example.

If one of my limiting beliefs is: "I'm not worthy of success,"

and I write my new belief as: "I am capable of being a millionaire next year,"

that's not going to sit well with me. That's too far of a reach.

So instead, let's try, "I am capable of success."

See how that still reverses the belief? It's a small step forward from the limiting belief, and it sits well with me because I can find evidence to support it.

Repeat this Mantra: I give up freely what is no longer serving me.

3 RELEASING OUR FEARS

I was once presented with the opportunity to speak in front of a large group over a topic that 1) I was completely comfortable with, and 2) was near and dear to my heart. I tentatively agreed, but with hesitation.

Why?

There was this nagging fear in the back of my mind. As time grew closer to having to make a final decision about whether or not to participate, my stomach was wrenched with dread. My mind flooded with all of these worries and fears. What if the audience doesn't think I know what I'm talking about? What is someone outwardly disagrees with me? What if I screw up?

After days of worry and internal turmoil, I turned down the gig. I then immediately began rationalizing my decision. I convinced myself the timing wasn't right, I had too many other things to do, I would miss the kids, and I was saving money by not going. The list went on and on, rationalizing my decision not to go, because that's what we do. When in reality, I let my irrational fears of rejection and disappointment control my decision-making ability. I also see this type of fear-based decision making over and over again with the clients I work with.

Fear is your body's natural way of keeping you alive. You are equipped with the instinct to protect yourself when you are faced with life threatening dangers. Your fight-or-flight response is trained to kick in, and you begin acting in an effort to protect yourself from death or bodily harm.

The challenge, however, is that over time our brain, essentially your ego, creates a sort of hack into this instinctive behavior. When this happens, fear then becomes the human motive for aversion, driven by your ego's need to keep you safe from *emotional discomfort*. Its sole purpose is to immediately release you from threat, strain, or pain—in other words, emotional discomfort. We as human beings have distorted our bodies' innate reaction to fear into a tool for feeling more emotionally comfortable, a crutch for emotional weakness.

Take a look at this list of actions. Each of these are an example of your ego in control, or your ego driving your decisions and your actions.

- You're easily offended.
- You gossip frequently.
- You're constantly searching for the next 'thing' that will make you feel good.
- You're unable to let go of the past.
- You draw your identity from roles and labels of society.
- You identify yourself based on your achievements.
- You worry about your reputation.
- You always need to be 'right.'
- You feel superior to others.
- You feel inferior to others.
- You compare yourself to others.

- You constantly complain about your situation or other people.
- You see yourself as a victim.
- You enhance your sense of self-worth through materialistic objects.
- You can't let go of situations when you've been wronged unless you feel vindicated.
- You blame your problems on other people or circumstances.
- You work from a scarcity mentality; there's never enough.
- You are always waiting for that next 'thing' to happen in order to feel content.
- You feel a sense of jealousy over other people's success.
- You function from a perspective of I, Me, Mine, and My.
- You have to 'win' an argument.
- You sulk when you don't win.

Our egos have distorted our bodies' innate reaction to fear. This distortion can be seen when we separate rational fears from irrational fears. As I previously mentioned, our bodies were designed with a true, instinctual fight-or-flight response to danger. It's designed to be a short-term response to an immediate, (life-threatening) rational fear. But, what's happened is we've created this hack into our system and manifested a long-term tool to avoid difficult situations, which are what I'm calling irrational fears.

Irrational fears are not real fears. Instead, you're simply avoiding rejection, judgement, abandonment, failure, and other types of emotional discomfort. Your ego is in control, creating all sorts of irrational fears that you then justify as rational fears in your mind. This is exactly what happened in my story where my ego had me convinced I would be rejected and labeled a fraud if I were to speak at that event. My irrational fear of judgement and failure kicked in my fight-or-flight response.

Irrational fears are simply your ego in control. Most of the fears you feel in life are simply a self-manifested anxiety that you've created to avoid emotional discomfort, that can be drilled down into two categories of pain: loss or hardship. When I say loss, this doesn't necessarily only refer to the physical loss of something or someone. It could be the loss of a sensation, a routine, or a pleasure.

For example, someone may not want to stop drinking every weekend with their friends because it boils down to the fact that they don't want to lose that sense of comradery they have with their friends. In terms of hardship, an example may be when a person won't quit a job or a relationship that they're absolutely miserable in because of the emotional discomfort it may cause in the short term. So once again, fear, driven by our ego, controls our actions.

I once worked with a client who struggled with letting go of her overbooked schedule. She came to me overwhelmed and exhausted from overcommitting herself. She struggled with saying no to commitments, even though she knew she was overwhelmed. After a few weeks of working through the underlying thoughts and beliefs behind this behavior, she uncovered an irrational fear that if she said no and created more space on her calendar that she would be seen as lazy. In her mind, her busy schedule and overwhelm were keeping her from the emotional discomfort she thought she'd feel by letting it go. Her ego had created an irrational fear that letting go of the overwhelm could equate to a loss of identity, a loss of being seen as a strong, driven woman.

Your ego has created irrational fears that control your actions. However, it's also crucial to know when these irrational fears started and when they've been justified in your mind. This is why doing the limiting beliefs activity in the previous chapter is so important. You have to know what your limiting beliefs are in order to understand which of your fears are irrational, and where they come from. This is why you must look to the past before you can ever change your present or future. This is why the Life Roadmap activity inside the Rock Your Happy program is THE single most valuable, and life changing activity that my clients experience in the program. That activity allows my clients to look at their life experiences from a 10,000 foot view. By doing this, they're able to pinpoint specific life experiences that attributed to their limiting beliefs. Mapping out an actual road map of their life allowed my clients to connect the dots and see exactly how they came to be where they're at today. It's an incredibly eye opening activity.

These irrational fears did not just pop up overnight, nor did it take one incident to solidify them. They have been interwoven throughout your entire life, in your past, to become what they are today. Events you experienced as a child, teenager, young adult, in relationships, careers, and with your family all led up to the irrational fears you have in place, which your ego then attempts to protect you from. The result? You start making fear-based decisions. You stay in a job you absolutely despise, you stay in a relationship that is toxic, you continue bad habits, you avoid tough conversations, and you turn down opportunities, all because you let fear control your decisions.

Life-Changing Action

Set a timer for 5 minutes. In your journal, or in the companion workbook available at www.jennifershreckengost.com/bookbonuses, write down ten significant decisions you have made in your life. These decisions may surround incidents such as:

- leaving/staying in a job

- leaving/staying in a relationship
- moving to a new area
- social events/interactions
- habits
- education
- friendships

Don't think, don't process, and don't give your brain time to step in and start rationalizing your decisions. Continuously write until the timer goes off.

Looking at your list of decisions, consider whether or not they were driven by fear. Use this example below to help you evaluate each decision.

Decision: I chose not to present at a conference I was invited to.

Was this driven by fear? Yes

Why? Because I didn't want anyone judging my knowledge, skills, or ability.

What was I fearing? Judgement

Why was I fearing this? I don't want to feel

judged by others. It makes me feel shameful, inadequate, and that I'm not good enough.

Was this an avoidance of loss, hardship, or emotional discomfort? Yes

Is this an irrational fear? Yes

As you go through this process, you should start to see fears popping up repeatedly. Make a list of all the irrational fears you identified that are driving your decisions. These fears may include:

- judgement
- shame
- inadequacy
- loneliness
- abandonment
- vulnerability
- failure
- loss

Whatever irrational fears showed up, write them all down.

In order to release your irrational fears, you get to walk yourself through a four-step releasing process.

Step One: Honor your current state

Step Two: Face your fears

Step Three: Ask why

Step Four: Reframe your fears

Step 1: Honor your current state

Before you begin to analyze and release all of the irrational fears that came up for you, you first get to take the time to honor where you are right now. The last thing I want for you is for your head to be filled with negative self-talk, beating yourself up for making fear-based decisions, or being overcome with feelings of shame, guilt, or regret.

I'll give you an example. *Self-affirmation: Every day, in every way I am learning to embrace my imperfections.* This affirmation honors your current state and honors your effort to embrace all of you, including your irrational fears.

Write down three self-affirmations that honor where you are right now. This simple step of honoring where you are now is crucial to creating new beliefs and releasing those irrational fears.

Step 2: Face your fears

It's time to face the music and call out your fears. From your list, identify your 3-5 strongest irrational fears that have controlled your decision making. I want you to sit with those 3-5 irrational fears and feel any emotions that come up when you read those words or visualize them in action.

Think of your fears as the Boogey Man under your bed when you were a kid. As you sat there in your dark room as a child, scared to death as you imagined the scary Boogey Man under your bed, you were paralyzed with fear. However, once you called him out, shined the light and declared he no longer scared you and admitted he wasn't real, he lost all of his power over you. It's the same with our fears. They're the scary Boogey Man under our bed that we need to call out, declare they're not real, and that they no longer have the power to control us.

Step 3: Ask why

It's time to go a little deeper with these fears and begin to ask why they really exist. For each of the fears you listed above, I want you to walk through a series of asking yourself why until you feel like you've reached the root of the fear. Remember, your ego is there to protect you from emotional discomfort. Even though you've called out your irrational fears that have been controlling our decisions, you might need to look a little deeper and uncover an even deeper layer.

See the below example:

Fear-based decision - Staying in a job I hated

What am I really afraid of? I'm afraid of leaving my job.

Why are you afraid of leaving your job? - Because I need steady income.

Why are you afraid of leaving your job? - Because people will think I'm irresponsible.

Why are you afraid of leaving your job? - Because my family will be disappointed in me.

Why are you afraid of leaving your job? - Because I'd be humiliated if I didn't succeed on my own.

Why are you afraid of leaving your job? - Because people will judge me if I'm not successful.

Why are you afraid of leaving your job? - Because I'll feel like a failure.

Why are you afraid of leaving your job? - Because I'm just not good enough to make it on my own.

Now we're at the root of that crippling irrational fear that's keeping you from moving forward. Imagine you and I sitting in a room together and me continually asking you, "Why?" For every response you give me, I continue to ask why, continue to ask you to go deeper. You'd probably get frustrated with me, right? This activity requires us to go deep, and requires us to threaten our ego that's trying to keep us safe. Don't stop at the surface level; frustrate yourself just as I would probably frustrate you by gently nudging you to go deeper. See what you can uncover.

Step 4: Reframe your fears

For each of your fears you've now uncovered, I want you to consider how you want to feel instead. Instead of having those fears control your decisions, what do you want to see happen instead? What do you want to feel instead? Write these down. Next, consider what actions you can take to begin feeling this way. How can you release the control of these irrational fears? What can you start doing today to reframe these fears into more positive, growth-based decisions? Allow yourself to feel this positive alternative, this reframing, with every sense: sight, smell, sound, feel, even taste. Feel the shift in your mindset around this. Visualize it as if it's happening.

Remember, just like with limiting beliefs, reframing your fears and letting go of their crippling grip is a gradual process. I'm arming you with tools that can help get you started, but know that it takes continual work. Just like with any other skill, practice makes perfect, so you get to continue to hone your skill set in order to break free from fear-based decision making. The goal is to move into a place of growth-based decision making, where your decisions are aligned with your core values, and they're all part of your plan towards reconnecting, realigning, and rediscovering you again. So, let's keep working.

Repeat this Mantra: I move beyond my old limitations.

4 EMBRACING VULNERABILITY

Just the thought of speaking the word **vulnerability** makes you tense up and throw up in your mouth just a little, right? All those fears and limiting beliefs we just spent three chapters on probably just came rushing back to the surface. You're probably thinking, "Dang, Jennifer! I just exhausted all of my emotions and energy getting to the root of my fears and limiting beliefs, and now you want me to embrace vulnerability?!?"

I get it, being vulnerable is TTOOOUUUGGGHHH stuff. Just hearing the word 'vulnerability' makes your ego pipe up like a night shift guard who just heard a noise down the hall. It knows vulnerability means emotional discomfort (in the beginning), and it is armed and ready to keep you safe.

Vulnerability is crucial if you truly want to reconnect and realign with your true self. Vulnerability not only allows you to be connected with others, but it also allows you to be connected with yourself. Until you're connected with yourself, you'll most likely be living your life for other people. Additionally, in order to set boundaries, ask for what you want, and advocate for yourself, you'll have to get vulnerable to do so.

Remember in the movie Jerry Maguire, when Tom Cruise's character, Jerry Maguire, goes running back to his wife, Dorothy, interrupts her women's group and says, "I'm not letting you get rid of me...You complete me." Dorothy cuts him off and says, "You had me at hello." This is vulnerability. Jerry asked for what he wanted, even though he could have been turned away or embarrassed by the other women in the room. Dorothy was also vulnerable when she cut him off and spoke the truth when she could have let her ego run the show and tell him off just to 'win.' We see scenes like this over and over in books and movies and we melt in our seats, longing to have that type of interaction in real life, but we're too afraid to actually be vulnerable enough to allow it to happen.

Vulnerability isn't just for romantic comedies and happy endings. Vulnerability is where you step into your true self and create an aligned life. It's when you tell your spouse what you need and don't need from them. It's when you say no to commitments that don't feel aligned with your goals or dreams, at the risk of judgement by others. It's when you show up as you, the real you, unfiltered picture and all. That's when the magic happens.

The challenge, however, is that being vulnerable, either with yourself or with others, is difficult. Your inability to be vulnerable in your relationships partly stems from a scarcity mindset. This is not scarcity in terms of material items, but scarcity within yourself. Your mind is flooded with thoughts of scarcity, as if you're never enough:

- never successful enough,
- never perfect enough,

- never skinny enough,
- never smart enough,
- never good enough

This scarcity mindset is interwoven within your stories propelled by shame, fears, and limiting beliefs. As a result, your actions become driven by what is commonly referred to as a hidden agenda.

Let's look at some very simple actions we see every day that women often take because they're stuck in a scarcity mindset:

- Earning degrees, certifications, etc. when they're not really necessary

- Throwing extravagant parties

- Posting selfies or pictures on social media

- Buying materialistic items we don't really need

Now let's look at these same actions through the hidden agenda lens:

- Earning degrees, certifications, etc. (to prove I'm smart, capable, and successful).

- Throwing extravagant parties (to gain the attention and validation from the guests; "wow, you really throw a great party!")

- Posting selfies or pictures on social media (to gain the likes, hearts, and other emoticons from your followers - self-validation).

- Buying materialistic items we don't really need (to be perceived with some sort of status, to feel good enough, wealthy, of a certain class).

Hidden agendas are driven by a shame-based fear. That fear ties directly back to a fear of being vulnerable. **Shame + Fear = Inability to be vulnerable**.

We're afraid of being ordinary.

We're afraid of feeling less than.

We're afraid of judgement.

We're afraid of that scarcity story in our heads.

Below is an exercise to help you understand your hidden agendas.

Complete the following sentence:

"I really need _____ because then I will finally be _____, prove_____, and feel_____"

Here's how you might fill that sentence out: "I really need to earn this promotion because then I will finally be seen as successful, prove to everyone I am capable of success, and feel accomplished." In that example, you're not getting the promotion because you want it, you're getting it to prove your worthiness to others wrapped up in a package of 'success.'

Or, what about, "I really need to throw an amazing Pinterest-worthy birthday party for my daughter because then I will look like a rockstar mom, prove to others how great life is and feel like a great mom. In that example, you're not throwing a birthday party to create a loving experience where family can be together and be present in the moment, you're doing it to create a perceived image and keep up with the Joneses.

If you're struggling to complete the above sentence, consider past or present actions that are driven by one or more of the three factors below:

- Driven by the need to feel a certain way: safe, free, successful, empowered

- Driven by the need to prove or have validation: smart enough, talented enough, skilled enough

- Driven by the need to become something: respected, known, recognized

By definition, vulnerability is the state of being exposed to the possibility of being attacked or harmed, either physically or emotionally. By allowing your hidden agendas, also known as fear-based shame, to drive your actions, you're avoiding vulnerability.

As humans, we each have unique vulnerabilities, some of which create a more intense reaction than others. Some states of vulnerability are tolerable; however, for most people there are two core vulnerabilities that trigger the strongest response and avoidance: fear and shame.

We already know how powerful fear's grip can be on us, so it should be no surprise that these should also be tied to vulnerability as well.

Fear Core Vulnerability is driven by a fear of isolation or deprivation.

This might look like:

- Staying in toxic relationships or friendships to feel connected
- Staying in terrible jobs to feel financially secure

Thoughts may be consumed with:

- "Sam won't love me anymore, or won't want to be with me."
- "I won't be able to buy nice things anymore."

Fear Core Vulnerability focuses on the

<u>hardship</u> created by a <u>loss</u>.

Shame Core Vulnerability is driven by a fear of failure.

This might look like:

- Risking abandonment to feel success (working long hours, putting their job above all else)
- Buying materialistic things to present a certain status quo
- Taking any and all measures to get a promotion

Thoughts may be consumed with ideas like:

- "If I lose my job people with think I'm a failure."
- "I couldn't show my face in public if I got a divorce."

Shame Core Vulnerability will focus on how we will look to other people when something is lost.

Consider these two types of vulnerabilities.

Which is your core vulnerability? Which triggers the deepest response and avoidance?

If you don't allow yourself to be vulnerable, then you're most likely falling short of creating that life you've been longing for. I'm going to go out on a limb and guess that you're a master at hiding that suffocating overwhelm. All of those thoughts you have swirling around in your head, thoughts about how you long for something to change…you're most likely keeping them to yourself. Am I right?

This is why embracing vulnerability is another key piece to reconnecting, realigning and rediscovering you again. No longer can you live in a bubble where you hide your wants, your dreams, and your struggles. No longer can you silently hide in the bathroom just wanting a break, then drive home in silence on your commute, begging for something to change. No longer can you hide your true feelings and needs deep down, bottling them up until it all becomes too much and you snap. It's time to get vulnerable, acknowledge what you truly want, set boundaries, and start advocating for yourself.

Life-Changing Action

You're going to test the waters with vulnerability by embracing vulnerability. As I mentioned before, vulnerability is like any other muscle. We must use it to strengthen it. But, the good news is, the more you try it, the easier it gets. Vulnerability starts to feel less and less uncomfortable, and it becomes easier to share what you're really feeling in the moment, helping you become the real you again.

Over the next week I want you to choose just ONE vulnerable action you can take and then reflect. Here are some examples:

- Share a shameful part of your story that's keeping you from moving forward with the change you desire.

- Be vulnerable with someone you trust and share something you're truly struggling with.

- Have a difficult conversation that you've been avoiding.

- Showcase your flaws, challenges, or fears.

- Ask for boundaries with your loved ones. This might be no interruptions after 8:00 pm so you can have time to yourself, or asking your husband to share in the pick-up duties so you can go to a yoga class.

When you avoid vulnerability, you're preventing yourself from living your truth, from living a life that sets your soul on fire, from reconnecting with the real you again. Let's start by baby stepping your way towards embracing vulnerability.

Repeat this Mantra: I choose to show the world the real me.

5 BUILDING A FOUNDATION OF SELF-LOVE, CARE, AND COMPASSION

A few years ago, I tracked everything I said to myself over the course of a week, and boy, was it an eye-opener. My inner mean girl, who I refer to as Regina (as in Regina George in the movie *Mean Girls*), was out. of. control. Tracking my thoughts and seeing them stare back at me in black and white was harsh. "OMG you look disgusting." "God, I look so old." "Fatty McFatterson." It was terrible.

If I actually spoke to someone else the way I spoke to myself I would be mortified, but yet here I was, saying these awful things to myself. Self-confidence can be a real B, and so many women struggle with not only self-confidence, but also showing themselves self-love, care, and compassion. Actually saying nice things to yourself or showing affection to yourself can almost feel uncomfortable if it's not something you regularly practice. In fact, I have had clients actually try to skip this module inside the Rock Your Happy program because it felt too uncomfortable for them.

You may have gone so far away from showing yourself self-love, care, and compassion that you've formed a strong aversion to the thought of it. I'm not talking about just getting weekly manicures and massages (which are still good for the soul). I'm talking about truly, deep down, loving yourself and everything about you. Consider your children. Your love for them runs so deep, it's like there's nothing they could ever do or say that would make you love them any less. This is how we should love ourselves. Love yourself with the same burning love that you have for your children.

Let's do a short visualization exercise. I'd like for you to sit back and close your eyes. Visualize a recent situation where you didn't feel very self-confident.

- What was happening?
- What were your surroundings?
- Who was with you?
- Are the people with you those that triggered your lack of self-confidence?
- What were you feeling then, both emotionally and physically, and what are you feeling now as you think about your experience?
- What was your instinct in this situation?
- Do you notice any connection to your previous fears or limiting beliefs resurfacing?

Here are a few additional signs that indicate poor self-confidence:

Body language: Defensive body language such as crossing your arms. This may also be tied to the actual behavior of being defensive verbally.

Reacting to criticism: The urge to immediately react to even the smallest criticism.

Overcompensating: Covering up conscious or subconscious weaknesses, frustrations, and/or feelings of inadequacy through gratification or striving towards perfection in another area.

Justifying your actions: Justifying your actions or mistakes rather than just accepting them as they are.

Blame: Blaming others around you rather than just accepting the situation as it is.

Perfectionism: Constantly striving towards perfection and not being content until you reach the set level of perfection. (Which, by the way, is a level you'll never reach.)

Does any of this feel familiar to you? Did you read any of these and think, "Oh snap, this is me!!"? It's okay if you did; it simply means you get to do the work to improve your ability to show yourself love, care, and compassion. Your level of self-confidence is directly tied back to the same fears and limiting beliefs you previously identified. Remember, it's your ego's job to keep you from emotional discomfort. If you're feeling a lack of self-confidence in areas like dating, career, body image, public speaking, etc., it's directly tied back to your ego protecting you from the emotional discomfort it THINKS you will endure, due to the fears and limiting beliefs sitting back in your subconscious.

Moral of the story: it's time to stop beating yourself up for your lack of self-confidence. Self-confidence isn't something you inherit, and it's also not a constant trait. To build your self-confidence you get to *continually* to do the work to release the fears, reverse the limiting beliefs, let go of expectations, and practice being vulnerable. Self-confidence is also like a garden. If you don't tend to your garden, it will begin to be taken over by ugly weeds, killing the beauty inside. However, if you weed your garden (clear out the fears and limiting beliefs), your garden will flourish.

The first step towards growing your self-confidence is through self-love and acceptance. This means loving and accepting yourself just as you are, honoring your needs, setting boundaries, and releasing your dependency on others' judgement and opinions. Tall order, huh? I promise you, it's possible.

I talk a lot about owning your stories when

I work with clients. Usually, when we get to self-love and self-confidence and how they're affected by your limiting beliefs and fears, there's also an element of shame involved. We all have stories from our past we'd rather forget and pretend they didn't happen. Until you fully claim them as part of who you are today, they'll continue to eat away at you, control you, and kill your self-love and acceptance. This is again why the Life Roadmap activity inside the Rock Your Happy program is so powerful. We lay it all out there, every single experience, interaction, relationship, no matter how good, bad, ugly, or dark. Once you do this, you can begin to heal and you can begin your journey towards self-acceptance.

Take a moment to do a temperature check on your level of self-love and acceptance. Take a look at the list below, and consider how often you find yourself engaging in any of the following behaviors:

- Being hypercritical of yourself
- Self-sabotage
- Difficulty with accepting compliments

- Never feeling as though you're enough
- Seeking external validation
- Not setting boundaries

If you want to take it a step further, for the next 24 hours, record your thoughts and words you say to yourself. Become aware of the words you use with yourself, along with your actions.

Your thought journal may look something like this:

"God, look at those gray hairs, ugh!"

"Oh I should post that picture, I look amazing!"

"Today I'm going to stay on track and eat healthy."

"I don't feel like a salad, let's do Chipotle today, it's not that bad."

"God, I feel so bloated.

"Okay, tomorrow I'm going to do a salad."

"Come on Jennifer, this shouldn't be that hard."

"My boss told me nice work on my project. I said thanks, but also listed off four reasons why it wasn't a big deal."

You get the idea?

This can be an eye-opening exercise, but also one that can bring negative emotions to the surface. What you don't want to do during this exercise is perpetuate the negative self-talk by talking negatively to yourself about your negative self-talk. That sounded like a tongue twister. But, I promise you, it's incredibly common! Simply record your thoughts and words you say to yourself, nothing more, nothing less. Do not judge yourself for your self-talk.

Life-Changing Action

I want to preface this life changing action section with a note regarding self-love and acceptance. Self-confidence and acceptance is extremely challenging for women. We tend to be so hypercritical of ourselves, and have moved so far past loving ourselves for who we are, that the idea of building our self-confidence muscle almost seems like an impossible task. The good news is, it's not impossible. However, it will take work and it will take time.

This is the number one challenge the women I work with face, yet it's one of the most important behaviors to change if you want to truly reconnect, realign, and rediscover you again. Below are four strategies for building your self-confidence, love, and acceptance muscle. These are not a magic pill. You won't miraculously drop all of the negative self-talk after a few rounds of these. It will take time, it will take self-compassion, and it will take patience. But, in the end, your self-acceptance will grow, even if it's ever so slowly.

Daily Gratitude

Keeping a daily gratitude journal allows us to express our gratitude for all the things we have rather than focusing on what we don't. In fact, keeping a daily gratitude journal is an integral part of the Rock Your Happy program.

Every night, end the day by listing what you're grateful for that day.

Then, write down 3 compliments to yourself.

End your journal entry with writing, "I receive that."

You'll be amazed at how far gratitude will take you.

Celebrate YOU

Choose a picture of yourself and print it out.

Tape or glue this picture onto one of your journal pages.

Below that picture, celebrate YOU by responding to each of the prompts below:

"Three things I am good at:"

"Things I'm really proud of:"

"I am unique because _____" (List out ways in which you are YOU)

"Three things I love about me:"

Lastly, read through each of these and be proud of YOU!

Squash the Negative Self-Talk

Self-affirmations are the quickest way to quieting your negative inner self-talk.

If you haven't already, create a list of self-affirmations that call to you. I recommend creating self-affirmations that negate your strongest limiting beliefs and fears. Once you have your list, take these self-affirmations even further by recording yourself reading them into a voice memo or as an mp3 file and upload into your iTunes playlist. The act of listening to these affirmations daily will help solidify them within your subconscious. Don't worry about what you sound like; that's your fears talking again! Embrace yourself, just as you are.

Separate from Your Emotions

When you begin to feel negative emotions and poor self-confidence, love or acceptance, disassociate yourself from the emotion. Just observe the situation and see what's happening as a separate event. Understand what's happening and why. Remove your emotions' power over you by seeing them as objects you can release, pass along, or push aside. By doing this, you'll be able to release the control of these negative emotions.

Reverse Self-Criticism

For each of your observed poor self-confidence, love, and acceptance behaviors you previously identified, write how you want to act and feel instead that would exhibit strong self-confidence, love, and acceptance. Describe these alternatives in detail so that you can begin to see how real they can be.

Start a Practice of Self-Care

Create a practice of self-care for the whole

you, that encompasses all five core life areas. Engage in activities that nurture and support all of you: Physical, Spiritual, Emotional, Personal, and Professional. My suggestion is to implement at least one form of self-care in each core life area weekly.

Self-Care Activities for Physical:

1. Eating nutritiously dense foods
2. Regular exercise or body movement (find what works for you)
3. Walking
4. Yoga
5. Swimming
6. Strength training
7. Biking
8. Running
9. Massage
10. Acupuncture
11. Reiki session
12. Soaking in an Epsom salt bath
13. Safe living environment

14. Routine medical care

15. Get 6-8 hours of sleep

16. Stay hydrated

17. Tune in to your sexuality

18. Meditate

19. Rest

20. Set boundaries and allow for 'me' time

These are just a few examples of how you can honor the physical core life area with self-care. What self-care activities can you begin to implement in the core life area of physical?

Self-Care Activities for Spiritual:

1. Meditate
2. Journal
3. Self-reflect
4. Engage in your spiritual community
5. Ground yourself with mother nature by engaging your bare feet with the Earth.
6. Go for a walk in nature
7. Pray
8. Play

9. Volunteer for a cause
10. Involve yourself in charitable actions
11. Explore essential oils either aromatically or topically
12. Do a saging ritual
13. Explore feng shui
14. Explore crystals
15. Reiki session
16. Turn off your cell phone and reduce screen time

These are just a few examples of how you can honor the spiritual core life area with self-care. What self-care activities can you begin to implement in the core life area of spiritual?

Self-Care Activities for Emotional:

1. Self-affirmations
2. Mirror work
3. Meditate
4. Laugh
5. Cry
6. Hug

7. Listen to music
8. Watch a funny show or movie
9. Practice forgiveness, self-love, and self-compassion
10. Conduct a release ritual to release negative emotions that no longer serve you
11. Journal
12. Write a letter to yourself outlining everything you love about YOU
13. Explore essential oils either aromatically or topically.
14. Gratitude journal

These are just a few examples of how you can honor the emotional core life area with self-care. What self-care activities can you begin to implement in the core life area of emotional?

Self-Care Activities for Personal:

1. Conduct a self-discovery exercise
2. Explore new hobbies
3. Revisit old hobbies
4. Learn a new skill

5. Let go of relationships or hobbies that feel forced
6. Foster relationships that feel good
7. Explore visualization activities
8. Meditate
9. Create an aligned vision board
10. Invest in yourself with programs or coaching
11. Set boundaries
12. Create space for play
13. Write out your perfect day
14. Journal

These are just a few examples of how you can honor the personal core life area with self-care. What self-care activities can you begin to implement in the core life area of personal?

Self-Care Activities for Professional:

1. Take time for lunch every day
2. Take breaks
3. Set boundaries

4. If you sit for longer periods of time, stand at least once every hour
5. Leave work at work
6. Do not work during scheduled time off
7. Learn to say NO
8. Take vacation time
9. Take sick time
10. Take a mental health day, if needed
11. If you're unhappy, begin to plan for something new
12. Understand your rights as an employee
13. Find a support network
14. Go for walks
15. Stay hydrated throughout the day
16. Stay fueled; don't skip meals

These are just a few examples of how you can honor the professional core life area with self-care. What self-care activities can you begin to implement in the professional core life are?

Repeat this Mantra: I let go of the negative feelings about myself, and accept all that is good.

6 ALIGNING WITH YOUR CORE VALUES

Every year in my corporate job, we would take a full day offsite to review our yearly strategic plans. This process also included reviewing our company mission statement and core values. As we worked to develop our strategic plan for the upcoming year, we went through several exercises to ensure that all of our goals and plans for the upcoming year's strategic plan were in fact aligned with the company's values. Everything we did inside that company had to be aligned with those two things: mission statement and core values.

It was a refreshing activity where we could

look to the future and plan for only those goals that were aligned with the core of our company. It allowed us to 'cut the fat' and not waste time, energy, and resources that weren't aligned with our core and where we wanted to take the company and/or department in the following year. When we knew exactly what the plan was, what the goals were, and it was all aligned with the mission statement and the core values, decision making was easy peasy. So, why don't we do this with ourselves as human beings?

It may sound weird, but identifying your core values is crucial for designing that life you've been longing for, a life where you feel connected, aligned, and balanced, where you feel as though you're living the life YOU want, not the life of others' expectations. If you're like me and you're a professional overthinker, having your core values in place also makes decision making easy as pie. If something isn't aligned with your core values, it's a no go. It's that simple. This module inside the Rock Your Happy program is by far the differentiator from other programs. Your core values are your epicenter. All things in life should revolve around these. You might also be asking yourself, "Well how in the world do I even begin to figure these out?" Don't worry, I'll baby step you through the process.

Let's start by choosing your core values. What the heck are core values? Core values are the fundamental beliefs of a person or organization. They are the guiding principles that dictate behavior, and they help you determine if you are on the right path towards fulfilling your goals by creating an unwavering guide. They form the foundation from which we perform work and conduct ourselves. They are built from our beliefs and from who we are as people.

In order to identify your core values, you must truly look at yourself and define who you really are. This will then lead you into identifying your core values.

Step One: Get crystal clear on who you are as a person

Step Two: Identify your core values

Understanding who you really are can be a scary place. It means learning about who you are, and what really matters to you, not who you *think* you should be or what *should* matter to you. This work comes from within, not from those around you. This means identifying, understanding, and cutting through values that someone else has given you so you can find the values that are actually yours.

When I started to define my core values, I started from a place of 'shoulds.' I chose thoughts and beliefs that I thought I *should* believe in and stand for, but that weren't truly aligned with who I really was. I had to keep asking myself, "Who am I?" and "Is what I'm doing right now in alignment with who I want to be?" Asking questions can help you say NO to what isn't right for you, and YES to what is. Doing this work allows us to begin living in alignment.

Consider the following:

- What excites you?

- What bores you?
- What does success look and feel like to you?
- What is failure?
- What do you fear the most?
- What makes you feel fulfilled?
- What is your brilliance?
- What makes you happy?
- What makes you sad?
- What makes you angry?
- What is your primary question in life?
- What's most important to you in your life?
- What else is most important to you in life?
- What's least important to you in life?
- What do you want from life?
- What's most important for you to avoid in life?
- What do you want your legacy to look like?

- What do you value?
- What do you despise?
- What hurts you?
- What lights you up?

These questions are the tip of the iceberg. When members of a company work to discover the company's core values, they must know who THEY are in order to best serve their customers and also grow and flourish. It's the same with yourself. You must know who you are, what you want, and how you want to feel in order to start living the life you want. From here, you can then begin the process of identifying your five true core values.

Life-Changing Action

Core Values

Now that you have an idea of who you are and what you want, you can begin to identify your core values. These core values are what will be the source of your alignment. They will drive your core-desired feelings in each of the five core life areas and lead you on your path towards living an aligned life where you feel like YOU again. This is where you begin to start creating the foundation from which you'll move forward.

For this activity, I have my clients use a list of values from Steve Pavlina, which you can access at https://www.stevepavlina.com/blog/2004/11/list-of-values/. I've also included the list here inside the book and in the companion workbook you can download at www.jennifershreckengost.com/bookbonuses.

To identify your five true core values, I'm going to walk you through a five-step process that will span over the course of four days. It's important to walk away from this activity and then come back to it, as taking time away from your list helps see it with a fresh mind and lessens the chance of Overthinking 101.

Day 1 - First pass: Review the list of values and delete what does NOT call out to you. This doesn't mean that it's not an important value; it simply does not feel instantly aligned, and that's okay.

Day 2 - Second pass: Review the remaining words on the list after day one and again delete additional words that do feel aligned.

Day 3 - Third pass: Now, narrow down your list to 20 values.

Day 4 - Choose 5 VALUES from those 20 that call to you as YOUR core values.

My Core Value 1:

My Core Value 2:

My Core Value 3:

My Core Value 4:

My Core Value 5:

Abundance

Acceptance

Accessibility

Accomplishment

Accountability

Accuracy

Achievement

Acknowledgement

Activeness

Adaptability

Adoration

Adroitness

Advancement

Adventure

Affection

Affluence

- Aggressiveness
- Agility
- Alertness
- Altruism
- Amazement
- Ambition
- Amusement
- Anticipation
- Appreciation
- Approachability
- Approval
- Art
- Articulacy
- Artistry
- Assertiveness
- Assurance
- Attentiveness
- Attractiveness
- Audacity
- Availability
- Awareness
- Awe
- Balance
- Beauty
- Being the best
- Belonging
- Benevolence
- Bliss
- Boldness
- Bravery
- Brilliance
- Buoyancy
- Calmness
- Camaraderie
- Candor
- Capability
- Care
- Carefulness
- Celebrity
- Certainty
- Challenge
- Change
- Charity
- Charm

Chastity
Cheerfulness
Clarity
Cleanliness
Clear-mindedness
Cleverness
Closeness
Comfort
Commitment
Community
Compassion
Competence
Competition
Completion
Composure
Concentration
Confidence
Conformity
Congruency
Connection
Consciousness
Conservation

Consistency
Contentment
Continuity
Contribution
Control
Conviction
Conviviality
Coolness
Cooperation
Cordiality
Correctness
Country
Courage
Courtesy
Craftiness
Creativity
Credibility
Cunning
Curiosity
Daring
Decisiveness
Decorum

Deference	Eagerness
Delight	Ease
Dependability	Economy
Depth	Ecstasy
Desire	Education
Determination	Effectiveness
Devotion	Efficiency
Devoutness	Elation
Dexterity	Elegance
Dignity	Empathy
Diligence	Encouragement
Direction	Endurance
Directness	Energy
Discipline	Enjoyment
Discovery	Entertainment
Discretion	Enthusiasm
Diversity	Environmentalism
Dominance	Ethics
Dreaming	Euphoria
Drive	Excellence
Duty	Excitement
Dynamism	Exhilaration

- Expectancy
- Expediency
- Experience
- Expertise
- Exploration
- Expressiveness
- Extravagance
- Extroversion
- Exuberance
- Fairness
- Faith
- Fame
- Family
- Fascination
- Fashion
- Fearlessness
- Ferocity
- Fidelity
- Fierceness
- Financial independence
- Firmness
- Fitness
- Flexibility
- Flow
- Fluency
- Focus
- Fortitude
- Frankness
- Freedom
- Friendliness
- Friendship
- Frugality
- Fun
- Gallantry
- Generosity
- Gentility
- Giving
- Grace
- Gratitude
- Gregariousness
- Growth
- Guidance
- Happiness
- Harmony

- Health
- Heart
- Helpfulness
- Heroism
- Holiness
- Honesty
- Honor
- Hopefulness
- Hospitality
- Humility
- Humor
- Hygiene
- Imagination
- Impact
- Impartiality
- Independence
- Individuality
- Industry
- Influence
- Ingenuity
- Inquisitiveness
- Insightfulness
- Inspiration
- Integrity
- Intellect
- Intelligence
- Intensity
- Intimacy
- Intrepidness
- Introspection
- Introversion
- Intuition
- Intuitiveness
- Inventiveness
- Investing
- Involvement
- Joy
- Judiciousness
- Justice
- Keenness
- Kindness
- Knowledge
- Leadership
- Learning

Liberation	Neatness
Liberty	Nerve
Lightness	Noncomformity
Liveliness	Obedience
Logic	Open-mindedness
Longevity	Openness
Love	Optimism
Loyalty	Order
Majesty	Organization
Making a difference	Originality
Marriage	Outdoors
Mastery	Outlandishness
Maturity	Outrageousness
Meaning	Partnership
Meekness	Patience
Mellowness	Passion
Meticulousness	Peace
Mindfulness	Perceptiveness
Modesty	Perfection
Motivation	Perkiness
Mysteriousness	Perseverance
Nature	Persistence

- Persuasiveness
- Philanthropy
- Piety
- Playfulness
- Pleasantness
- Pleasure
- Poise
- Polish
- Popularity
- Potency
- Power
- Practicality
- Pragmatism
- Precision
- Preparedness
- Presence
- Pride
- Privacy
- Proactivity
- Professionalism
- Prosperity
- Prudence
- Punctuality
- Purity
- Rationality
- Realism
- Reason
- Reasonableness
- Recognition
- Recreation
- Refinement
- Reflection
- Relaxation
- Reliability
- Relief
- Religiousness
- Reputation
- Resilience
- Resolution
- Resolve
- Resourcefulness
- Respect
- Responsibility
- Rest

- Restraint
- Reverence
- Richness
- Rigor
- Sacredness
- Sacrifice
- Sagacity
- Saintliness
- Sanguinity
- Satisfaction
- Science
- Security
- Self-control
- Selflessness
- Self-reliance
- Self-respect
- Sensitivity
- Sensuality
- Serenity
- Service
- Sexiness
- Sexuality
- Sharing
- Shrewdness
- Significance
- Silence
- Silliness
- Simplicity
- Sincerity
- Skillfulness
- Solidarity
- Solitude
- Sophistication
- Soundness
- Speed
- Spirit
- Spirituality
- Spontaneity
- Spunk
- Stability
- Status
- Stealth
- Stillness
- Strength

- Structure
- Success
- Support
- Supremacy
- Surprise
- Sympathy
- Synergy
- Teaching
- Teamwork
- Temperance
- Thankfulness
- Thoroughness
- Thoughtfulness
- Thrift
- Tidiness
- Timeliness
- Traditionalism
- Tranquility
- Transcendence
- Trust
- Trustworthiness
- Truth
- Understanding
- Unflappability
- Uniqueness
- Unity
- Usefulness
- Utility
- Valor
- Variety
- Victory
- Vigor
- Virtue
- Vision
- Vitality
- Vivacity
- Volunteering
- Warmheartedness
- Warmth
- Watchfulness
- Wealth
- Willfulness
- Willingness
- Winning

Wisdom	Worthiness
Wittiness	Youthfulness
Wonder	
	Zeal

There you have it! Your five true core values. *Note: if there is a sixth value that you simply don't want to leave off, you can go ahead and add it. But do not choose more than six core values and do not have less than five.* Everything you do in life, every decision you make, every opportunity you pursue, every relationship you build, should all be aligned with one or more of these core values. When you base the decisions in your life on your core values, you will be well on your way to living in alignment and designing a life that sets your soul on fire.

Keep your list of core values somewhere close and easily accessible, like on a card in your wallet or on a sticky note right above your desk. Make sure you can refer to your list during times when you're having difficulty deciding whether an action is aligned with your values. Over time, you'll find that you memorize your values, and incorporating them into your everyday life will become second nature.

Repeat this Mantra: I boldly go in the direction of my dreams.

7 DESIGNING THE FRAMEWORK FOR ROCKING YOUR HAPPY!

At this point you might be thinking, "Now what? I know my core values. I have tools in my toolbox to combat fear and limiting beliefs when they pop up, so I should wake up tomorrow living my fulfilled life, unapologetically rocking my happy, right?" Well, not quite, but the puzzle pieces are almost all put together.

Years ago, I made a giant list of all the things I wanted in life. Think of a vision board, if you will. On this vision board I cut out and pasted pictures of trips I wanted to take, things I wanted to do, hobbies I wanted to learn, etc. After the board was all nice and finished, I said to myself, "Okay, Jennifer. As soon as the kids graduate, you lose 50 pounds, you have $100,000 in savings, and you pay off all debt, THEN you can enjoy this vision board." Guess what happened? There was always another 'have to' that I put in front of everything before I could actually BE or DO any of those things listed on my vision board. I was functioning from a fixed mindset of HAVE-BE-DO rather than a growth mindset of BE-DO-HAVE.

BE, DO, HAVE

Three powerful words, used often by Zig Ziglar.

You must **BE**, before you can **DO**, then you will **HAVE**.

Seems easy enough right?

The challenge is that most of us, my old self included, function in the **HAVE, DO, BE** mindset.

If you're functioning with a **HAVE, DO, BE** mindset, it might look something like this:

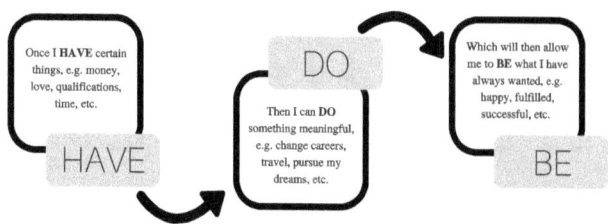

When you're functioning in this mindset, you are again driven by a scarcity mindset. You think, or at least you've convinced yourself, that you cannot **DO** the things you desire or **BE** that person you want to be until you **HAVE** certain things. When you're in the **HAVE-DO-BE** mindset you're also usually making fear-based decisions rather than growth decisions. Rarely will you ever reach the **BE** phase because you'll always be waiting for the **HAVE**. In my situation, I kept waiting until I crossed off all the **HAVES** before I ever got to **DO** or **BE**. This cycle continued and that vision board slowly gathered dust before meeting its demise one day when I gave up on it all.

Instead of thinking in the **HAVE-DO-BE** mindset, I needed to think from a **BE-DO-HAVE** mindset, or growth mindset. **BE-DO-HAVE** mindset would look something like this:

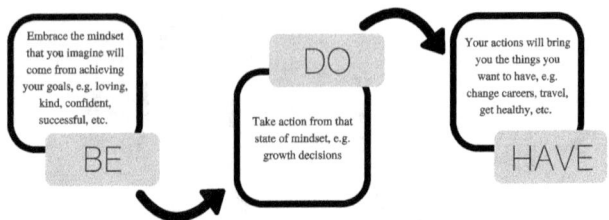

Most people believe if they **HAVE** (e.g. more time, more money, more business), then they can finally **DO** (e.g. write a book, take up a hobby, go on vacation, buy a home, expand their business), which will allow them to **BE** (e.g. happy, peaceful, successful, etc.).

Example: HAVE, DO, BE

"If I HAVE a lot of money, then I could DO what I want and I'd then BE successful."

This is an example of a victim mindset. In this instance, you're constantly waiting for external situations to change before you can have or achieve what you want in life

Let's reverse this into BE, DO, HAVE statement.

Example: BE, DO, HAVE

"I am a confident and successful business owner (BE). Every day I complete tasks that push me

towards success (DO). I have a successful business (HAVE).

This is an example of a growth mindset. In this instance, it's not what you have to have in order to get what you want. You become the type of person you need to be to access the outcomes you want. Then you consider what types of actions that person would be doing and start doing them. The haves just naturally come because of your actions and you fully trust that the haves will happen.

Example: "If I lose 20 pounds (HAVE), then I could go on a vacation to the beach (DO) and then I'd be healthy and happy (BE)."

Let's reverse this into a BE, DO, HAVE statement.

"I am confident, happy and healthy. I love myself as I am and engage in activities that make me feel happy and healthy. I don't stress about losing weight, I focus on being healthy, happy and loving who I am."

Example: "If I HAVE more time, then I can DO the things that make me happy, and then I'll finally BE rocking my happy!

Let's reverse this into a BE, DO, HAVE statement.

"I am happy and carefree (BE); I find joy in everything I DO. I am happy and fulfilled (HAVE)."

Starting with HAVE means you're stuck in the victim mindset. You're stuck in an endless cycle of not being able to be or do the things you want until you have something, and when that doesn't happen (which most of the time it won't), you play the victim with why you're not getting results. "I can't be confident because I haven't lost the weight," or "I can't experience life because I don't have a lot of money," etc. Consider your own mindset in the past. Have you been functioning in the **BE-DO-HAVE** framework, or the **HAVE-DO-BE**?

Let's try an exercise to help you shift to your new mindset. Identify a **HAVE-DO-BE** mindset you may have exhibited in the past.

HAVE-

DO-

BE-

Now try reversing this into **BE-DO-HAVE** process: (use the example from above to help you)

BE –

DO –

HAVE –

The good news is we can always change our mindset. By embracing the positive **BE** mindset from the start, you're setting yourself up for success. Rather than hanging your hopes of being happy and fulfilled on something actually having to happen, you get to *choose* to feel that way now.

BE: Be what you want now, whether it's happy, successful, confident, etc.

DO: Once you start acting as if you are what you want, then you will naturally start doing things that kind of person (happy, successful, confident, etc.) would do.

HAVE: Once you are being and doing what you've always wanted, the things you've always wanted to HAVE will start to fall into place.

It's the old "fake it till you make it" idea. Act successful and you will start adopt behaviors of success, which will then lead to you achieving success. **BE-DO-HAVE** will help you tap into the creative power of the Universe and propel you toward your goals.

Life-Changing Action – Part I

How do you know what you want to **BE, DO,** and **HAVE**? Remember your core values? Those are your epicenter. Everything comes from those. You rock your happy, align, and reconnect with your true self from those values. But, you need to break them down into manageable areas. If you recall way back in the introduction of this book, I had you write down three adjectives for each of the five core life areas within the Rock Your Happy program:

- Personal
- Emotional
- Spiritual
- Physical

- Professional

Those adjectives represented how you currently felt in each of those areas. Now that you've done the brave work and started getting clearer on what you really want inside your balanced and fulfilled life, it's time to identify your *new* core desired feelings. Designing your life around your core desired feelings creates a situation where you are living in alignment with your core values.

For each of the five core life areas, begin to identify adjectives that describe how you want to feel in each area. This is your BE of the BE-DO-HAVE mindset. I've provided you with a lengthy adjective list on the next few pages, so feel free to work from these or come up you're your own words. You're going to go through this activity again over the course of several days. The reason behind doing it this way is because people tend to answer questions with their logic brain first. Their logic brain quickly answers with what it thinks *should* be the right answer, rather than thinking more deeply from the heart and soul.

Take some time over the next few days and consider how you want to {FEEL} in each of these five core life areas. Use the list of adjectives here inside the book, or download the companion workbook at www.jennifershreckengost.com/bookbonuses.

Day 1 - First pass: Looking at the list of words, start crossing off words that immediately turn you off. It doesn't mean that they're bad, they're just not words that align with you or how you want to feel.

Day 2 - Second pass: Review the remaining words, then again go through and start crossing off words that don't feel aligned.

Day 3 - Third pass: Begin to circle words that you feel drawn to. You might even make a note of which core life area you'd like to feel this within.

Day 4 - Final Selection: Choose three adjectives for each of the five core life areas that honestly describe how you want to feel in each of those areas. You can have cross-over between the life areas, but make sure you're being honest and not going the easy route.

A

abandoned
able
absolute
adorable
adventurous
academic
acceptable
acclaimed
accomplished
accurate
aching
acidic
acrobatic
active
actual
adept
admirable
admired
adolescent
adorable
adored
advanced
afraid
affectionate
aged
aggravating
aggressive
agile
agitated
agonizing
agreeable
ajar
alarmed
alarming
alert
alienated
alive
all
altruistic
amazing
ambitious
ample
amused
amusing
anchored
ancient
angelic
angry
anguished
animated
annual

another
antique
anxious
any
apprehensive
appropriate
apt
arctic
arid
aromatic
artistic
ashamed
assured
astonishing
athletic
attached
attentive
attractive
austere
authentic
authorized
automatic
avaricious
average
aware
awesome

awful
awkward

B

babyish
bad
back
baggy
bare
barren
basic
beautiful
belated
beloved
beneficial
better
best
bewitched
big
big-hearted
biodegradable
bite-sized
bitter
black
black-and-white
bland

blank
blaring
bleak
blind
blissful
blond
blue
blushing
bogus
boiling
bold
bony
boring
bossy
both
bouncy
bountiful
bowed
brave
breakable
brief
bright
brilliant
brisk
broken
bronze
brown
bruised
bubbly
bulky
bumpy
buoyant
burdensome
burly
bustling
busy
buttery
buzzing

C

calculating
calm
candid
canine
capital
carefree
careful
careless
caring
cautious
cavernous
celebrated

charming	compassionate
cheap	competent
cheerful	complete
cheery	complex
chief	complicated
chilly	composed
chubby	concerned
circular	concrete
classic	confused
clean	conscious
clear	considerate
clear-cut	constant
clever	content
close	conventional
closed	cooked
cloudy	cool
clueless	cooperative
clumsy	coordinated
cluttered	corny
coarse	corrupt
cold	costly
colorful	courageous
colorless	courteous
colossal	crafty
comfortable	crazy
common	creamy

creative
creepy
criminal
crisp
critical
crooked
crowded
cruel
crushing
cuddly
cultivated
cultured
cumbersome
curly
curvy
cute
cylindrical

D

damaged
damp
dangerous
dapper
daring
darling
dark
dazzling
dead
deadly
deafening
dear
dearest
decent
decimal
decisive
deep
defenseless
defensive
defiant
deficient
definite
definitive
delayed
delectable
delicious
delightful
delirious
demanding
dense
dental
dependable
dependent

descriptive
deserted
detailed
determined
devoted
different
difficult
digital
diligent
dim
dimpled
dimwitted
direct
disastrous
discrete
disfigured
disgusting
disloyal
dismal
distant
downright
dreary
dirty
disguised
dishonest
dismal

distant
distinct
distorted
dizzy
dopey
doting
double
downright
drab
drafty
dramatic
dreary
droopy
dry
dual
dull
dutiful

E

each
eager
earnest
early
easy
easy-going
ecstatic

edible
educated
elaborate
elastic
elated
elderly
electric
elegant
elementary
elliptical
embarrassed
embellished
eminent
emotional
empty
enchanted
enchanting
energetic
enlightened
enormous
enraged
entire
envious
equal
equatorial
essential

esteemed
ethical
euphoric
even
evergreen
everlasting
every
evil
exalted
excellent
exemplary
exhausted
excitable
excited
exciting
exotic
expensive
experienced
expert
extraneous
extroverted
extra-large
extra-small

<u>F</u>

fabulous

failing	few
faint	fickle
fair	filthy
faithful	fine
fake	finished
false	firm
familiar	first
famous	firsthand
fancy	fitting
fantastic	fixed
far	flaky
faraway	flamboyant
far-flung	flashy
far-off	flat
fast	flawed
fat	flawless
fatal	flickering
fatherly	flimsy
favorable	flippant
favorite	flowery
fearful	fluffy
fearless	fluid
feisty	flustered
feline	focused
female	fond
feminine	foolhardy

foolish
forceful
forked
formal
forsaken
forthright
fortunate
fragrant
frail
frank
frayed
free
French
fresh
frequent
friendly
frightened
frightening
frigid
frilly
frizzy
frivolous
front
frosty
frozen
frugal

fruitful
full
fumbling
functional
funny
fussy
fuzzy

G

gargantuan
gaseous
general
generous
gentle
genuine
giant
giddy
gigantic
gifted
giving
glamorous
glaring
glass
gleaming
gleeful
glistening

glittering
gloomy
glorious
glossy
glum
golden
good
good-natured
gorgeous
graceful
gracious
grand
grandiose
granular
grateful
grave
gray
great
greedy
green
gregarious
grim
grimy
gripping
grizzled
gross
grotesque
grouchy
grounded
growing
growling
grown
grubby
gruesome
grumpy
guilty
gullible
gummy

H

hairy
half
handmade
handsome
handy
happy
happy-go-lucky
hard
hard-to-find
harmful
harmless
harmonious

harsh
hasty
hateful
haunting
healthy
heartfelt
hearty
heavenly
heavy
hefty
helpful
helpless
hidden
hideous
high
high-level
hilarious
hoarse
hollow
homely
honest
honorable
honored
hopeful
horrible
hospitable

hot
huge
humble
humiliating
humming
humongous
hungry
hurtful
husky

I

icky
icy
ideal
idealistic
identical
idle
idiotic
idolized
ignorant
ill
illegal
ill-fated
ill-informed
illiterate
illustrious

imaginary
imaginative
immaculate
immaterial
immediate
immense
impassioned
impeccable
impartial
imperfect
imperturbable
impish
impolite
important
impossible
impractical
impressionable
impressive
improbable
impure
inborn
incomparable
incompatible
incomplete
inconsequential
incredible

indelible
inexperienced
indolent
infamous
infantile
infatuated
inferior
infinite
informal
innocent
insecure
insidious
insignificant
insistent
instructive
insubstantial
intelligent
intent
intentional
interesting
internal
international
intrepid
ironclad
irresponsible
irritating

itchy

J

jaded
jagged
jam-packed
jaunty
jealous
jittery
joint
jolly
jovial
joyful
joyous
jubilant
judicious
juicy
jumbo
junior
jumpy
juvenile

K

kaleidoscopic
keen
key
kind
kindhearted
kindly
klutzy
knobby
knotty
knowledgeable
knowing
known
kooky
kosher

L

lame
lanky
large
last
lasting
late
lavish
lawful
lazy
leading
lean
leafy
left

legal	lovely
legitimate	loving
light	low
lighthearted	loyal
likable	lucky
likely	lumbering
limited	luminous
limp	lumpy
limping	lustrous
linear	luxurious
lined	
liquid	**M**
little	mad
live	made-up
lively	magnificent
livid	majestic
loathsome	major
lone	male
lonely	mammoth
long	married
long-term	marvelous
loose	masculine
lopsided	massive
lost	mature
loud	meager
lovable	mealy

mean
measly
meaty
medical
mediocre
medium
meek
mellow
melodic
memorable
menacing
merry
messy
metallic
mild
milky
mindless
miniature
minor
minty
miserable
miserly
misguided
misty
mixed
modern

modest
moist
monstrous
monthly
monumental
moral
mortified
motherly
motionless
mountainous
muddy
muffled
multicolored
mundane
murky
mushy
musty
muted
mysterious

N

naive
narrow
nasty
natural
naughty

nautical
near
neat
necessary
needy
negative
neglected
negligible
neighboring
nervous
new
next
nice
nifty
nimble
nippy
nocturnal
noisy
nonstop
normal
notable
noted
noteworthy
novel
noxious
numb

nutritious
nutty

O

obedient
obese
oblong
oily
oblong
obvious
occasional
odd
oddball
offbeat
offensive
official
old
old-fashioned
only
open
optimal
optimistic
opulent
orange
orderly
organic

ornate
ornery
ordinary
original
other
our
outlying
outgoing
outlandish
outrageous
outstanding
oval
overcooked
overdue
overjoyed
overlooked

P

palatable
pale
paltry
parallel
parched
partial
passionate
past

pastel
peaceful
peppery
perfect
perfumed
periodic
perky
personal
pertinent
pesky
pessimistic
petty
phony
physical
piercing
pink
pitiful
plain
plaintive
plastic
playful
pleasant
pleased
pleasing
plump
plush

polished
polite
political
pointed
pointless
poised
poor
popular
portly
posh
positive
possible
potable
powerful
powerless
practical
precious
present
prestigious
pretty
precious
previous
pricey
prickly
primary
prime

pristine
private
prize
probable
productive
profitable
profuse
proper
proud
prudent
punctual
pungent
puny
pure
purple
pushy
putrid
puzzled
puzzling

Q

quaint
qualified
quarrelsome
quarterly
queasy

querulous
questionable
quick
quick-witted
quiet
quintessential
quirky
quixotic
quizzical

R

radiant
ragged
rapid
rare
rash
raw
recent
reckless
rectangular
ready
real
realistic
reasonable
red
reflecting
regal
regular
reliable
relieved
remarkable
remorseful
remote
repentant
required
respectful
responsible
repulsive
revolving
rewarding
rich
rigid
right
ringed
ripe
roasted
robust
rosy
rotating
rotten
rough
round

rowdy
royal
rubbery
rundown
ruddy
rude
runny
rural
rusty

S

sad
safe
salty
same
sandy
sane
sarcastic
sardonic
satisfied
scaly
scarce
scared
scary
scented
scholarly

scientific
scornful
scratchy
scrawny
second
secondary
second-hand
secret
self-assured
self-reliant
selfish
sentimental
separate
serene
serious
serpentine
several
severe
shabby
shadowy
shady
shallow
shameful
shameless
sharp
shimmering

shiny
shocked
shocking
shoddy
short
short-term
showy
shrill
shy
sick
silent
silky
silly
silver
similar
simple
simplistic
sinful
single
sizzling
skeletal
skinny
sleepy
slight
slim
slimy

slippery
slow
slushy
small
smart
smoggy
smooth
smug
snappy
snarling
sneaky
sniveling
snoopy
sociable
soft
soggy
solid
somber
some
spherical
sophisticated
sore
sorrowful
soulful
soupy
sour

Spanish
sparkling
sparse
specific
spectacular
speedy
spicy
spiffy
spirited
spiteful
splendid
spotless
spotted
spry
square
squeaky
squiggly
stable
staid
stained
stale
standard
starchy
stark
starry
steep

sticky
stiff
stimulating
stingy
stormy
straight
strange
steel
strict
strident
striking
striped
strong
studious
stunning
stupendous
stupid
sturdy
stylish
subdued
submissive
substantial
subtle
suburban
sudden
sugary

sunny
super
superb
superficial
superior
supportive
sure-footed
surprised
suspicious
svelte
sweaty
sweet
sweltering
swift
sympathetic

T

tall
talkative
tame
tan
tangible
tart
tasty
tattered
taut

tedious
teeming
tempting
tender
tense
tepid
terrible
terrific
testy
thankful
that
these
thick
thin
third
thirsty
this
thorough
thorny
those
thoughtful
threadbare
thrifty
thunderous
tidy
tight

timely
tinted
tiny
tired
torn
total
tough
traumatic
treasured
tremendous
tragic
trained
tremendous
triangular
tricky
trifling
trim
trivial
troubled
true
trusting
trustworthy
trusty
truthful
tubby
turbulent

twin

U

ugly
ultimate
unacceptable
unaware
uncomfortable
uncommon
unconscious
understated
unequaled
uneven
unfinished
unfit
unfolded
unfortunate
unhappy
unhealthy
uniform
unimportant
unique
united
unkempt
unknown
unlawful

unlined
unlucky
unnatural
unpleasant
unrealistic
unripe
unruly
unselfish
unsightly
unsteady
unsung
untidy
untimely
untried
untrue
unused
unusual
unwelcome
unwieldy
unwilling
unwitting
unwritten
upbeat
upright
upset
urban

usable
used
useful
useless
utilized
utter

V

vacant
vague
vain
valid
valuable
vapid
variable
vast
velvety
venerated
vengeful
verifiable
vibrant
vicious
victorious
vigilant
vigorous
villainous

violet
violent
virtual
virtuous
visible
vital
vivacious
vivid
voluminous

W

wan
warlike
warm
warmhearted
warped
wary
wasteful
watchful
waterlogged
watery
wavy
wealthy
weak
weary
webbed
wee
weekly
weepy
weighty
weird
welcome
well-documented
well-groomed
well-informed
well-lit
well-made
well-off
well-to-do
well-worn
wet
which
whimsical
whirlwind
whispered
white
whole
whopping
wicked
wide
wide-eyed
wiggly

- wild
- willing
- wilted
- winding
- windy
- winged
- wiry
- wise
- witty
- wobbly
- woeful
- wonderful
- wooden
- woozy
- wordy
- worldly
- worn
- worried
- worrisome
- worse
- worst
- worthless
- worthwhile
- worthy
- wrathful
- wretched
- writhing
- wrong
- wry

Y

- yawning
- yearly
- yellow
- yellowish
- young
- youthful
- yummy

Z

- zany
- zealous
- zesty
- zigzag

How do you feel about your new core desired feelings? These, along with your core values and are your new epicenter, the core of who

YOU are and what you want to BE.

Life-Changing Action – Part II

Visualizations are powerful exercises that are practiced by some of the most successful people in the world. Elite athletes, top leaders, and peak performers all utilize the practice of visualization. When you visualize what you want as if you already have it, and visualize it so clearly that you can feel yourself living that life, you can rapidly accelerate your achievement of those dreams, goals and ambitions.

Visualization activates the Law of Attraction, triggers your subconscious, and adds an extra boost of drive behind your internal motivation. When you visualize having the life you've always wanted, you can begin to see, hear, feel, taste, and touch what that life would be like. Now that you have identified your core values and core desired feelings, it's time to start visualizing what your happy, balanced, and fulfilled life will look like.

Here's a visualization I want you to try:

- Find a quiet spot, where you can sit uninterrupted for 10-15 minutes. Have your journal, something to write with, and a timer nearby.

- Remove all noise and distractions.

- Sit in a comfortable position, close your eyes and begin to relax.

- Set a timer for 10 minutes.

- Begin to visualize your core values and your core desired feelings. Think about the BE-DO-HAVE mindset.

- Visualize what life is like when you're FEELING those core desired feelings in each area.

- Visualize what life is like when you get to BE what you've been desiring.

- Visualize what life is like when you get to DO what you've been longing to do.

- Visualize what life is like when you get to HAVE those things you desire, that are aligned with your core values.

- Allow yourself to just visualize what life would be like inside your most fulfilled life.

When the timer goes off after 10 minutes, turn to your journal and write about your new happy and fulfilled life. Write what a typical day would be like. Extend that vision into a typical month, or even a typical year. Remember to draw from your five senses. What are you seeing, feeling, hearing, tasting, and touching inside your fulfilled life? Describe YOU. What do you get to BE-DO-HAVE inside your fulfilled life? Let your writing flow for as long as you want; there is no right or wrong. This becomes the narrative for your soul. This is your NEW story. This is you, rocking your happy, reconnected and realigned with the real YOU again!

Repeat this Mantra: As I maintain a detailed picture of what I desire, I automatically bring that desire towards me.

8 SETTING YOUR GOALS FOR MOVING FORWARD

It's time to CELEBRATE!! If you made it to the end of this book then you are one of the brave ones, doing the brave work that many people are too scared to face. You may have cried, laughed, been frustrated and exhausted, but you've also been enlightened along the way. You most likely uncovered parts of your story you may not have wanted to, but you pushed on because you knew that reconnecting, realigning and rediscovering you again to create a happy and balanced lifestyle was a non-negotiable.

YOU ARE BRAVE!

And for that it's time to celebrate YOU!

So, take some time, my friend, to do just that, to celebrate YOU! Go for a walk, visit your favorite coffee shop, meditate, buy a cute new journal, buy a new book; just do something that is just FOR YOU. You've earned it.

At this point of the book, you're also at the make-or-break point for long-term success. You're at a fork in the road. One road leads you towards long-term success; the other leads you right back to where you started. We are masters at consuming information. In fact, it's easier to spend our time consuming new information than to actually implement, revisit, and the implement again. You can either add this book to your bookshelf, never to revisit again, or you can get intentional AF and put these skills and strategies into action, revisiting when you need realignment, and continuing your path towards happiness, balance, and fulfillment.

I used to be the master at consuming information. I read every personal development book they ever published (or so it felt). I took courses, attended workshops, signed up for programs, and listened to podcasts, I consumed IT ALL! I consumed 90% of the time and only ever implemented about 10%. It was much easier to stay in the consuming lane, because actually implementing the work meant I had to face all the scary shit: fears, limiting beliefs, guilt, regret, etc. If I just consumed, I could still play it safe and *pretend* I was doing the work. Right?

You owe yourself to do more than just play it safe.

You uncovered your fears and limiting beliefs that have been holding you back.

You embraced vulnerability and began the work to grow your self-confidence.

You identified your core values and your core desired feelings.

All of this work is designed to create the solid platform from which you can go out and start rocking your happy from a place of alignment! Be the REAL YOU and love every minute of it!

So which path will you choose? Will you shove this book onto your bookshelf and move on, never actually implementing any change? Or will you put what you've learned here into action and continue to learn, implement, learn, implement? If you're ready to get intentional AF, start creating you most fulfilled life, and live in alignment with your core values and core desired feelings, then it starts with setting goals.

*A little note about intentions vs. goals. Intentions are in the present moment. You don't plan how to get there, you just intend the outcome and surrender the process, the HOW part of the journey, to the Universe. You've already done this work through your chosen core values and desired feelings. This is your BE statements. Goals are focused on the future. They're the **DO** part of the **BE-DO-HAVE**. You know how you want to feel in each of your core life areas. Now it's time to set tangible goals you can take aligned action towards.*

Life-Changing Action

Referring to the work you've done thus far, and working from a **BE-DO-HAVE** mindset, it's time to set your goals and intentions for moving forward.

Long-Term Goals

Long-term goals require time and planning. These are goals that are usually years in the future. Considering your core values and core desired feelings, visualize three to five long-term goals you'd like to achieve and write them down.

Note: When we begin to set long-term goals for ourselves, when we push towards change, this is when our ego kicks fear into action. Doubt and fear will start to kick in and you'll start talking yourself out of your goals. Use the process below to help you keep fear at bay when setting your long-term goals. Think of your goals as if they have already happened. Don't get sucked into the tube of worry.

Day 1 - First pass: Write down three to five long-term goals you would like to achieve, including the timeframe by which you will achieve them. (1 year, 3 years, 5 years)

Day 2 - Second pass: Review your initial goals. If you're hesitant on any of the goals ask yourself:

1. Is this aligned with my core values?

2. Is this aligned with my core desired feelings in that area?

3. Is irrational fear coming up?

Day 3 - Third pass: Solidify your three to five long-term goals and the timeframe by which you will achieve them.

Short-Term Goals

Short-term goals are goals that can be achieved in the near future, usually one year or less. Short-term goals are often, but not always, building blocks towards achieving long-term goals.

Considering your core values, core desired feelings, and long-term goals, visualize three to five short-term goals you'd like to achieve and write them down. *Remember, be aware of when fear is kicking in.*

Day 1 - First pass: Write down three to five short-term goals you would like to achieve, including the timeframe by which you will achieve them (days, weeks, months).

Day 2 - Second pass: Review your initial goals.

If you're hesitant on any of the goals ask yourself:

1. Is this aligned with my core values?

2. Is this aligned with my core desired feelings in that area?

3. Is irrational fear coming up?

Day 3 - Third pass: Solidify your three to five short-term goals and the timeframe by which you will achieve them.

Accountability

Setting goals is one step, but actually implementing and taking action is another. It's the difference between someone who takes a dozen online courses or reads a dozen books, but does nothing to actually apply what they just learned, and someone who actually gets out there and applies that knowledge. It's the difference between someone who says she wants to eat healthy and goes out and collects a bunch of healthy eating recipes and the person who actually starts to fuel her body with high-quality food. It's the difference between the woman who talks about how much she'd love to travel to Europe and the woman who actually books her plane tickets.

What's the big difference between these women? Accountability. When you have someone or something holding you to your goals, you're more likely to follow through on them. This is why so many New Year's resolutions and other goals fail: we don't have enough accountability, or the right kind of accountability. I want to make sure that you actually reach those goals you've painstakingly identified.

How will you stay accountable? Below are just a few examples of how you can stay accountable:

- Identify an accountability partner you can check in with on your progress.

- Focus on your mindset, and keep up with daily mindset practices.

- Frequently revisit your core values and core desired feelings. Make sure you're staying in a place of alignment.

Accountability can seem like an easy, throw-away step, but I promise you, making sure that you have a plan to stay accountable is going to be the difference between success and letting your goals and dreams fall to the side. You are so incredibly close to getting the life you love. Make sure you have the accountability you need to actually get there.

Repeat this Mantra: I am committed to being focused on my goal. I am worth it.

10 SO, NOW WHAT?

We just solved all the world's problems, right? Not quite, but we did just stock your personal toolbox with some serious tools to keep you on the path towards designing a life that sets your soul on fire. There's no one-size-fits-all for this; your happy, fulfilled life is as unique as your DNA. Your fulfilled life connects directly back to YOUR core values and core desired feelings. You'll need to continually weed your mindset garden and keep the tools in your toolbox sharpened because your fears and limiting beliefs *will* resurface. There is no magic pot of gold at the end of the rainbow. There's only awareness, intention, and alignment. Be aware of your emotional triggers and do the mindset work in order to work through those triggers quickly before they fester. Live with intention, choosing only those activities, relationships, and opportunities that allow you to live in alignment with your core values and core desired feelings.

The content of this book is an appetizer to the full Rock Your Happy program. Inside the Rock Your Happy, you'll take a deeper dive into some of these same activities within this book, plus more, including the transformational Life Roadmap Activity and the Release Ritual. Those two activities inside the program are by far the most popular with previous clients due to the sheer fact that they are the most eye-opening and transformational.

> *"The moment I realized just what the Rock Your Happy program was helping me to accomplish was during the Fear module. This module awoke the only skepticism I had felt in the program, but it turned out to provide the most impact of all of the modules. I literally felt a weight I had been*

carrying for so long lift during the Release Ritual and felt I really could become an active participant in my life again. That activity was life-changing for me."

– Mallory, Rock Your Happy graduate.

You will also get one-on-one coaching with me inside the Rock Your Happy Program, which takes the program from simply an online course to being a transformational experience. I help you process the emotions and triggers that come up. I ask the hard questions in a safe environment. I walk with you as you unlock your stories and learn to accept all of you.

You're proud of the life you've worked so hard for, yet, something just feels off. You're vaguely dissatisfied with life but you just can't quite pinpoint exactly what the problem is.

You feel like you're spinning in circles, reading the next personal development book, trying the next "right" step, but it's just not working. Then you beat yourself up with negative self-talk thinking, "Why can't I just be happy?!"

It's like a mirage. Every time you get closer to finally feeling content and balanced, it continues to be just out of reach.

On the outside you look like you've got your shit together; you're one badass mamma crossing tasks off our to-do list like no other. You're taking care of everyone, doing all the things. People even praise you for how well you "balance" life.

But it doesn't feel that way on the inside.

You feel disconnected and overwhelmed. You feel a bit lost, like you've lost YOU after years of wearing all the name badges: mom, wife, boss, friend, etc.

You're functioning on autopilot. You're stuck in a cycle of trying to find the magic fix to finally reach that pinnacle of happiness, balance, and fulfillment. Life feels a bit like Groundhog Day, rinse and repeat. Eventually autopilot stops working and things come to a crashing halt.

The problem is you're looking in all the wrong places. You're looking for the answers on the outside: books, podcasts, articles, but the answers all lie on the inside, within your understanding of how your past stories and experiences make you whole. You'll feel empowered and in control of your internal dialogue, with the ability to make growth decisions that propel you forward in life. You'll embrace a loving and appreciative relationship with yourself through development a practice of self-care and compassion. You'll understand your core values and desired feelings in all areas of life, while learning how to set boundaries, ask for what you want, and advocate for yourself without fear or shame.

"Before the program, I felt like I didn't know myself, and I felt somewhat dissatisfied with my life and relationships and like I was struggling with my internal thoughts and internal/external expectations. I felt like I was going in circles… constantly thinking and wondering and trying to understand myself and getting nowhere. The more pressure I put on myself the worse I felt. Just kind of internally spinning, spinning, spinning and making myself sick. Jennifer is open, honest, kind and non-judgmental. She

gave me a safe space to be brutally honest without fear. And she's good at getting me to see things I couldn't see before, although she rarely spells it out for you... she guides you to get there and see it yourself! Without question I would recommend the Rock Your Happy program to other women. Do yourself a favor and do the work. It's hard, but so worth it!"

– Laura, Rock Your Happy graduate.

If you're ready to continue with this deep work and work side by side with me inside the Rock Your Happy Program, you can learn more about the program at https://jennifershreckengost.com/online-programs/. There you can find detailed information about the program.

Repeat this Mantra: I am worthy of investing in myself.

ABOUT THE AUTHOR

Jennifer is on a mission to empower high-achieving women to release the overwhelm in order to create a more balanced lifestyle. After spending 20 years pushing her way up the corporate ladder, she realized that she was chasing a mirage. What she thought would bring her satisfaction in life: the career, the title, the salary, the degrees, the recognition, was slowly killing her. She realized she wasn't living in alignment with how she truly wanted to feel and it was throwing her entire life off balance.

- Stress
- Overwhelm
- Anxiety

These are the silent killers of high-achieving women.

Making the decision to let go of the overwhelm and the alpha-female, masculine mindset and step into a more balanced lifestyle was the best decision she ever made. She wants to empower other high-achieving women to also release the overwhelm and create a more balanced lifestyle.

It's time to reconnect, realign, and rediscover YOU again!

You can connect with Jennifer on social media, through email, or via her website:
Website: www.jennifershreckengost.com

Facebook: https://www.facebook.com/jennifershreckengostcoaching/

Instagram: https://www.instagram.com/jennifershreckengost

Email: connect@jennifershreckengost.com

Jennifer also hosts a weekly podcast, Rock Your Happy, a weekly podcast all about helping women become their own happiness guru. Jennifer, along with special guests, dives into topics that support the whole woman: mind, body, and soul. Happiness is an inside job, so listen in and gather up all the tools you need to reconnect, realign, and rediscover YOU again! You can subscribe and listen to the podcast on Apple Podcasts, Stitcher, Google Play, Spotify, and TuneIn, or find all episodes at jennifershreckengost.com/podcast/

www.ingramcontent.com/pod-product-compliance
Lightning Source LLC
LaVergne TN
LVHW051600070426
835507LV00021B/2686